Something New Every Day
LETTING YOUR IMAGINATION TAKE FLIGHT

By Chantel C. Lucier

Copyright © 2018 The AtHome Experience
Content © 2018 by Chantel C. Lucier

First edition published in the USA in 2018
by The AtHome Experience

All rights reserved. No part of this book may be reproduced or utilized, in any form or by any means, electronic or otherwise, without written consent of the author or publisher.

The author and publisher of this book do not dispense medical advice nor do they prescribe the use of any of the exercises in this book as a form of treatment for any medical condition. This book is exploratory in nature and shared to awaken the individual to the present moment and, in so doing, aid in spiritual and emotional well-being.

Santa Rosa, CA

Book cover and art illustrations by Jasmin Garcia-Verdin
jgvillustrations.com
Photos and recipes by Chantel C. Lucier
TheAtHomeExperience.com

ISBN: 978-0-578-42390-6

Dedication

I dedicate this book to anyone who has ever been scared to step into the unknown. And to my grandmother, who was the quintessential doer and created art every day.

Contents

Acknowledgments	i-ii
Welcome	1-2
The Beginning	3-5
Day One: Noticing the signs	6-8
Day Two: Smile, Smile, Smile	9-11
Day Three: Plan a Trip	12-14
Day Four: From Disorder, Order	15-17
Day Five: I'm In No Rush	18-20
Day Six: That's Amore	21-22
Day Seven: Art is Everywhere	23-24
Day Eight: Try a New Vegetable	25-26
Day Nine: Put Your Body into It	27-28
Day Ten: I'm in Such a Pickle	29-32
Day Eleven: Play an Instrument	33-34
Day Twelve: The Road Less Traveled	35-36
Day Thirteen: Teatime	37-38
Day Fourteen: Get Out of the House	39-41
Day Fifteen: Discover a New Poet	42-44

Day Sixteen: Don't Look Down	45-46
Day Seventeen: Medicinal Makings	47-49
Day Eighteen: Enter a Church	50-52
Day Nineteen: Chewing Meditation	53-54
Day Twenty: Won't You Be My Neighbor	55-56
Day Twenty-One: Dealer's Choice	57-58
Day Twenty-Two: Make Bread	59-60
Day Twenty-Three: Paying Homage	61-62
Day Twenty-Four: Take a Hike	63-64
Day Twenty-Five: Sound Mapping	65-66
Day Twenty-Six: Art and Sky	67-68
Day Twenty-Seven: Ya'dig	69-71
Day Twenty-Eight: Nature Persists	72-73
Day Twenty-Nine: Wabi-Sabi	74-76
Day Thirty: Six Degrees	77-78
Afterword	79-85
Links & References	86
About the Author	87

"Do one thing every day that scares you."

- Eleanor Roosevelt

Acknowledgements

Family, friends, neighbors, strangers, because of you this human experience is one evolving mosh pit of growth and profundity.

Thank you John Miller for your undying attention to the everyday. For your humor and your ease and your friendship.

Thank you Alicia Nosenzo. Your life and attention to your work and career have inspired me countless times (plus we all know the food at your restaurants were often the subject of my "something new!").

Thank you Eve Proper for introducing me to the idea of doing something new every day – my life is forever changed.

Thank you Valeriana, my incredible mother, for being so generous of spirit and always sharing your abundant love. Thank you daddy-o, aka dad or Michael, for your contagious energy and adventurous heart.

Thank you Jasmin Garcia-Verdin. You are an incredible artist and illustrator. Your energy and attention to this book fills my heart. Your passion and fun spirit is contagious and I am ever-grateful.

Thank you MaKaye, my beautiful grandmother, you angel with turquoise wings. You taught me how important it is to bring people together, to not judge, and to cook for a tribe that is beyond your given family. Thank you for teaching me to be "a sunbeam."

To the love of my life, Zac Tucceri, who was taken way to soon, but because of this, probably gave me more inspiration to live and feel and cry and really be present every day.

To the people, the plants, the ocean, and the thrill of the first time. To a new cocktail, and a really bad meal because it seemed like a good idea at the time and it was definitely something new. Thank you to all my friends in Washington Heights, New York. I return to you again and again for inspiration, laughs, and love.

Thank you Mestre Ombrinho and the Capoeira Angola Quintal community. Savitri D. and the Stop Shopping crew. Thank you Jane Selle Morgan, Kate Thompson, Wendy Taylor, Denice Kondik, Lynn L'Archeveque Mullen, Bonnie Thomas, Cabernet Lazarus-Gavin, Kristen Kentner, Molly Chanoff, Deanne Sweidan, Laconia Koerner, Theadora Tolkin, Pat Coleine, Belinda Irons, Sharon B. Montgomery, Jessie Meegan, Adetola Abiade, Gigi Guiette, Dino Pantazopoulos, Timothy Williams, Michelle Skaer Therrien, Shannon Service, Holly Lynn Ellis, Brian Seibert, Ricardo Valdez, Karen Conroy, Maeve Yore, Julia Carr, and Shane Austin Kramer. Your friendships run deep and my love for you is ever-growing, however near or far we are from each other. It is your friendship that gives me the inspiration to feel and love and write.

Thank you to every aspect of life that persists and is always asking me to take notice. Every bird, every glance, every daily growth in the garden. To faces, new and old. To the regulars and the newbies. Thank you, thank you, thank you. It is for you that I write this book.

"There's a whole wide world outside my door,
To touch, taste, feel, and explore.
I will open it wide and step outside,
As my Soul is ready for more."

– Kaypacha (1)

Welcome!

Greetings, you mystic wanderer, you seeker of new things. I say hello from here, from this ledge, this precarious spot that finds me each day wondering what's next. This book is about exploring new experiences. A little nudge to ask "what if?"

Every day, for thirty days, I invite you to open to a chapter, in any order, and follow the prompt to try something new. There are three stages to each daily experience: 1) read; 2) do; and 3) record what you discover.

You might think, you have no time, but I urge you to abandon that belief for thirty days. You may have done some of these things before. If so, I encourage you to do them anyway and see how this time might be different. A beginner's mind will be needed here. A great ballet dancer knows a beginning class offers a host of challenges no matter what "stage" you are at or on.

So, let's take a leap into the unknown! This leap will send a jolt through our nervous system that can ultimately change the way we think and live.

Okay, let's get a little sciencey for a moment. When we do new things we're flexing and expanding our brain. By expanding I mean there are literally new cells communicating with one another and there are significant benefits to that new communication. New neural connections keep the brain active. So, new experiences = new connections. Changes to our internal and external environments give our brains the ability to build and reorganize these new connections. The incredible flexibility that occurs in the brain when doing something new births a sort of magical awareness. Like turning on a switch, the world figuratively begins to brighten.

The prompts in this book are based on experiences I had in doing something new every day. While I've had almost sixteen hundred to date, I offer you thirty to introduce you to this new way of walking through your life. Through these experiences may you learn more about the parts of you that are open and the parts of you that are closed. Through these exercises may you feel stretched and strengthened and renewed.

May this book help you get into the stagnant places within so that you may feel freed up! May you exit your comfort zone and enter the world with a fiercely open mind and heart. May you see openly, clearly, and in full color.

The Beginning

On August 3, 2014, I took on a challenge to try something new every day. I had committed to thirty days but was excited and hopeful I'd make it to one hundred before I ran out of things to do. To my surprise, not only did I go past thirty days, it's now many years later and I'm still delighted and invigorated to experience new things every day.

When I first started to do something new every day I was obsessed (and convinced) that it had to be something truly new. I went to obscure streets, ate a hundred year old egg, traveled near and far, and spent a pretty penny when I didn't always have one. I soon realized doing something new wasn't always a new place and it certainly didn't require me to spend any money. It became seeing something from a new perspective. Becoming more aware of things I had witnessed probably on a daily basis but never fully experienced before. Suddenly, even seeing my cat on an exercise ball or witnessing a light shining a little brighter on a flower I had walked past time and again brought me into greater contact with the present moment. It was "as if" it was the first time. The challenge was and remains - to be present right now. One-Moment-At-A-Time.

This daily ritual has truly changed my life. Sometimes it's simply a new flavor, a different path, baking bread for the first time, a piece of street art I haven't noticed before, or really good ramen. Other times, it's an unexpected occurrence that shakes me into becoming more present. In these moments, I feel a little piece of my old self fall away to make room for my new self. A self that is more... well, more here.

Committing to doing something new every day has changed my perspective on how I see my days. Days are no longer governed by what I have to do. Of course, they are that too, but they are something more. Every day I have to find something new, no matter how busy I think I am. And, if you know me, you know I keep busy! Every day I have to ask, what will I do different today? This question requires me to drop down into my body and become fiercely present. I can't always research and plan a new thing. More often than not I have to rely on being awake enough to witness the new experience. If I'm not, the experience will often slap me into existence. Like keisaku, in Zen Buddhism, where a teacher might slap the student with a wooden stick (often translated as "awakening stick"). It's a Zen slap! A slap to say, "wake up", "be aware", "become present!" The Zen slaps are fewer now, as I tend to be more keenly aware of everything around me. Every tree, every sound, every person passing by.

But there is something else that urges me on. I enjoy trying new things. I enjoy feeling more awake and alive. But there is another layer that feels even more important. In my work as a reflexologist, I've seen people who have been given death sentences live. I've seen people survive and thrive after being diagnosed with cancer or diabetes or a host of other diseases in the body. Disease is dis-ease, a lack of ease somewhere in the body. We can free up blockages. This is true scientifically and energetically.

When we shift our attention and intention on how we

experience our daily lives we give our inner bodies the opportunity to relax into the unknown. We become curious about the moment. We are no longer governed by what we know. We suspend hardened beliefs and become fully present to the ever-evolving now.

By taken ourselves out of our habitual routines we will experience the dis-ease in our bodies dissolve and the peaceful, present moment emerge.

So, delve in, sweet adventurer, this is your time. There is no expiration date, though death beckons, life too calls. May your heart, mind, and body feel stretched. May you have renewed energy. May a sense of inspiration and well-being pervade. May whatever is hard soften and whatever is separate feel integrated after this journey. Doing something new every day has changed my life, I hope it changes yours.

Walked the Brooklyn Bridge
August 3, 2014
DAY 1

DAY ONE

Noticing the Signs

We are accosted with signs all day, every day. And by signs, I mean literal signs. If you drive, take the bus, or ride the train you get more than your share.

Today, instead of feeling bombarded by the insistent advertisements telling you what you should buy, feel, do or see, reframe your perspective and discover what the messages might be saying to you specifically.

Years ago a friend of mine was thinking about moving but wasn't sure. One day, still heavy in thought and perplexed whether or not to leave, he looked up and saw a huge sign that read his last name followed by the word "moving". It was probably a moving company – but it was also his very unique last name! A sign not to be ignored.

See what the signs offer up to you today. The messages may be subtle or might seem to have no relevance at all. Soften your expectations. Perhaps it'll just be a little humor to begin your day.

Whatever it is, take note, jot it down, snap a photo, and consider what, if anything, is illuminated for you today.

Remember signs can be anywhere, even on a cereal box. They could also come in the form of an image or a heart shaped rock on a walking path.

Signs and symbols are always there. They offer up possibilities and we give them meaning. Or perhaps they're little love notes from our angels.

If you've done this sort of exercise before or want to beef up your experience, add this element: upon arising today meditate on one question that you would like an answer to. Write it down. As you travel through your day take note of the signs that stand out. See if the signs have answers for you.

I encourage you to look lightly, relax into your day, be aware of your thoughts, and see what the sign angels have to say.

JOURNAL

Signs - (stereo talk) Finn
9 attitudes as a meditation.

The 9 attitudes are mostly too tough for me mindfulness beyond meditation

Beginners Mind - I get it told with private meditation but not with mindful thought in meditation yet done in actual situations

nonjudgment - I work on that frequently as I do a powerful emphasis on power lot. First thought of into my expressed mind in a new situation - is it good or bad
she/no

acceptance - Don't even allow myself the pleasure of knowing what that could mean

Sunday I will use 9 attitudes to fill my personal meditation time. I look forward to that

Light now I am scared of mindfulness deep over the threshold

Question to answer - I'd like an answer for How to be mindful w/o threat.

DAY TWO

Smile, Smile, Smile

In 2015 the Dalai Lama spoke at an Action for Happiness event in London. He said, "my practice when I see someone, is to smile". (2)

So, for today, the offering is simple: smile, smile, smile. Not for a minute, not for an hour, but literally throughout your day.

In the shower: smile; making breakfast: smile; washing dishes: smile; on the train: smile; in traffic: smile; meeting the eyes of a passerby: smile; at your job: smile; and on and on.

A smile is contagious, the more we do it, the more we have a smile within that grows. And the more we smile at others the more they will pass it on.

People may not smile back (especially if you live in a big city). We are not accustomed to people smiling at us. There are approximately 10-12 small muscles associated with smiling so if you're not used to it prepare to be sore. Start the trend and strengthen those smiling muscles.

Onward, smilers! I'm curious how you'll feel today. Different, worse, better, the same? Take note of what comes up, inside and out. Carve a little time out at the end of your day to write about your experience. Now, GO!

"We shall never know all the good
that a simple smile can do."

- Mother Teresa

DAY THREE

Plan a Trip!

According to a 2010 study published in the journal Applied Research in Quality of Life, "just planning or anticipating your trip can make you happier than actually taking it."(3)

So, let's start here: where do you want to go? Near? Far? Anywhere! This is an exercise. We are merely planning, so all stops out. Choose your dream vacation, your perfect place. Is it visiting your grandkids cross-country? Is it going to some obscure beach off Fiji? Wherever your heart desires.

If you don't know where you want to go, start a list of things you'd like to see or experience. Do you want to be beachside? Near family? Near great food? What type of food? What's the perfect weather like?

Once you've narrowed down what you're looking for begin your search.

How you plan is up to you. For me, it's choosing a place and looking at ticket prices first. For some of you this might seem awful. Cutting out pretty pictures and contacting friends that live near that special place might be better for you. The way my mind works is I want to know what I am looking at financially. From there I start to find deals, then I start to imagine bringing in the money to afford it. Once I have that reality principal in place then I start dreaming. Pictures and places to go start to fill my day.

Whatever course you decide to take is yours. And who knows, you may even find a place and a time of year that is just right and you'll get a trip out of the exercise too. Journey on!

"Without leaps of imagination or dreaming,
we lose the excitement of possibilities.
Dreaming, after all is a form of planning."

- Gloria Steinem

JOURNAL

DAY FOUR

From Disorder, Order...

We all have that part of our room or home that is untidy. Perhaps a junk drawer or a pile we keep saying we'll go through. Well, today is your day!

Today, take an hour (just one hour) to clean. If you have more time or get inspired, by all means, carry on. But an hour is all that is needed.

I encourage you to go to a place that feels stagnant. While dishes and laundry might seem easier, go instead to the area you've been putting off. Is it in a corner, a drawer, or on the floor? There may even be something very important in there – but you won't know until you drudge.

There IS a correlation between our bodies and our homes. And where there is back up in our space there may also be backup in our lives. Sometimes our bodies will even reflect it. Think of it like this, clean the corners of your home and your colon too will be cleansed. Dust and polish pieces and your brain too will feel brighter. Gaze and ponder at heirlooms that are meaningful and your heart too will swell.

Take the time today for you. Your space. Your home or your office. When you journal, reflect on how your body felt before, during, and after.

"We are used to cleaning the outside house, but the most important house to clean is yourself - your own house - which we never do."

- Marina Abramović

JOURNAL

DAY FIVE

I'm in No Rush

Do you ever feel like you're in a rush even though you have nowhere pressing to go? For instance, do you find yourself anxious to get out of the office, off the plane, off the bus?

States of mind become habitual. It's part of what occurs in the brain when we do something again and again. Thoughts and actions are recorded and imprinted. Like fish downstream, the habitual thoughts, behaviors, and actions recur almost automatically.

In the movie "What the Bleep do you know" the lead character realizes her thoughts are creating stagnancy (and redundancy) so she actively creates new thoughts to break herself of the chains. In so doing, the neurotransmitters along the synaptic cleft went from traveling down one highway again and again to creating new grooves and thus, new thoughts.

It might feel strange to walk slowly or counterintuitive to take a break, do it anyway. Just for today, do not rush.

"Once you stop rushing through life,
you will be amazed how much more life
you have time for."

- Author Unknown

JOURNAL

DAY SIX

That's Amore!

When I lived in New York, I would have an annual pizza party every December. I'd invite all my friends, acquaintances, and people from the neighborhood. There would always be about a hundred people that would come at some point during the night to commune and partake. Luckily people would come at different times to accommodate my small New York cardboard box apartment.

Because this was an annual occurrence, and I'm a lover of new things, each year there would be departures into unknown pizzas. A tuna fish pizza, an Indian inspired pie, a pizza with every mushroom I could find.

Today, make a pizza. You can make it from scratch or get a pre-made dough. But the toppings should be fresh and inspired by what you love or would like to try.

What's your pizza?

JOURNAL

DAY SEVEN

Art is Everywhere

Living mostly in cities all my life, I am always walking briskly past beautiful street art. Today your challenge is to slow down and open your eyes to the art around you. If you live in a city this may be easier, but wherever you are, there is art.

I encourage you to shift your perspective of what art is. Maybe you have opinions about street art. Maybe you find it appalling or crude. Well then, this exercise is for you! This exercise won't ask you to change your perspective, it only asks that you suspend judgment long enough to take in what someone created. Open your heart and bear witness to the art that is all around.

Take time today to find and observe the art that occupies your streets. Take time to stroll mindfully and slowly. Take in the art. Find a piece that moves you, or disturbs you, or brings you joy, Write about your reflections. What does this piece bring up. What does your mind say? What does your heart speak? Enjoy the free street museum that is all around.

JOURNAL

DAY EIGHT

Try a New Vegetable

There are so many veggies available to us. No matter how remote you are, there is at least one you haven't tried. You may be accustomed to sticking to your favorites. Today try a veggie you've never eaten! Here's one I tried on February 21, 2016.

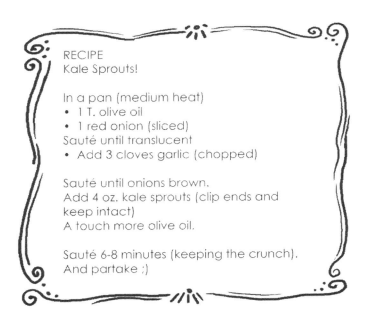

RECIPE
Kale Sprouts!

In a pan (medium heat)
- 1 T. olive oil
- 1 red onion (sliced)

Sauté until translucent
- Add 3 cloves garlic (chopped)

Sauté until onions brown.
Add 4 oz. kale sprouts (clip ends and keep intact)
A touch more olive oil.

Sauté 6-8 minutes (keeping the crunch).
And partake ;)

DAY NINE

Put Your Body into It

Today, do a physical activity you have never attempted. If you do yoga regularly, try something else. There are so many things. If you're at a loss, do a little investigating. Tai Chi in the park, swing dance at a local dance studio, skateboarding with a borrowed board from the kid next door, Qi gong, capoeira, surfing.

If you feel strapped for cash or worry about not having the time to go to that evening salsa social, look up an introductory video on-line. There are myriad exercise videos you can do for free!

If you have the time, choose something that propels you into public space. There are indoor and outdoor exercise excursions. Perhaps try the one you've always wanted to try but said you didn't have the time.

JOURNAL

DAY TEN

I'm in Such a Pickle

Oftentimes, when things are all stirred up and seemingly out of control, we need only divert our attention and give ourselves a task. That isn't to say we ignore what's happening, we just set it aside for a moment and put our attention on something else. It's kind of like having a disagreement with someone and having the courage to pause or sleep on it before you say something you'll regret.

This exercise is at once an opportunity to make something you've never made as well as an opportunity to task it up amidst whatever crazy might be going on in your life. A slight diversion can sometimes remedy a heavy heart or a crazed mind.

So today, do something, make something… perhaps pickles! Get creative. Give yourself over to the task and while you're at it, make it delicious! Here are a few recipes to wet your appetite, should you decide to actually make pickles!

RECIPE
Quick(ish) Pickled Red Onions
- 6 small organic red onions (thin half moons)
- 1 T fresh cilantro (chopped fine)
- 1 t. fresh flat parsley (chopped fine)
- 2 cups white vinegar
- 2 T apple cider vinegar
- 2 T maple syrup
- 2 T olive oil
- 1/2 t. crushed red pepper
- 2 pinches Celtic sea salt
- 10 cracks pepper

Put everything in a jar, stir well, let stand for an hour, place contents of jar in a pot (covered) at a low heat. Once the water gets hot (not boiling), take off heat, cool to room temperature and partake.

RECIPE
Pickled Chayote & Cucumbers
- 2 cups Vinegar
- 3 1/2 T Sugar
- 1-2 smashed Garlic Cloves
- 1 teas Whole Peppercorns
- 1 teas Red Pepper Flakes
- 1 teas Celtic Sea Salt

Cook on Stove - Simmer until sugar dissolves
Add 2 cups water
SLICE
- 2 French Cucumbers
- 1 Chayote
- 1 Jalapeño

Place in jar, pour brine, put lid on and into the fridge. Ready in 1-5 days.

RECIPE
Raw Pickled Beets

- 6 beets (deskinned & sliced thin)
- 1 small yellow onion (sliced thin)
- 1 garlic clove
- 2 cups white vinegar
- 2 cups water
- Just under a 1/2 cup org. sugar
- 1 teas. peppercorns
- 1/2 teas. red pepper flakes
- 1/2 teas. coriander seeds
- 1 teas. celtic sea salt

In a pot, boil water, vinegar, sugar, salt and spices.

Slice beets and onion like thin little moons, a whole clove of garlic and place in tall glass jar.

Once liquid gets hot pour over beets.
Let stand until it hits room temp. then cover with tight lid and place in fridge.

Ready in 5 hours to 5 days.

DAY ELEVEN

Play an Instrument

Today, play an instrument. If you're a musician, try one you haven't tried before. Along the same lines as building new muscles, new patterns of thought, and developing new neural pathways – go flex that music muscle!

There are many ways to get your hands on a new instrument. Most require little or no money at all. Here are a few options:
- Borrow one.
- Know a child? Give their keyboard, mini drum set, or other child instrument a go!
- Go to a music store and test one out.
- Find and take a music class.
- Dust off that instrument you told yourself you always wanted to play.
- Create an instrument using household items.
- In Marin and Sonoma County there are pianos in various outdoor locations. Does your area have a similar offering?

JOURNAL

DAY TWELVE

The Road Less Traveled...

One of the habits I find hardest to break is the habit of how I get places. We take the usual highway, the same exit, the familiar streets.

I have felt the most alive when on a vacation and don't know where I'm going. I've felt most serene when, on a day off, I decide to take a stroll in an unfamiliar part of town.

There's a calm and curiosity that pervades in these moments. But we don't have to be on vacation or even have a day off to experience the internal bliss of a new route.

Today take a different course. If you usually drive, take the train instead. If you usually walk, turn right instead of left. Give yourself a little more time than usual, and if at all possible, get lost. In this, you will surely be found!

JOURNAL

DAY THIRTEEN

Teatime

Today make a cup of tea of coffee or some other warm drink.

Keep all your attention on the process of creating and experiencing. Notice the subtleties of flavor. Can you identify the different flavors? Experience the taste on different parts of your tongue. Notice the change in temperature. Contemplate the color. Notice what thoughts come in, if any. And drink it as if it's your first time.

"Where there's tea there's hope."

- Arthur Wing Pinero

JOURNAL

DAY FOURTEEN

Get out of the House!

Ok, ok, I understand you might not be able to swing a show on a whim but there are infinite activities out there. They are beckoning you to come out and play. If you absolutely cannot do something tonight, do a little research and return to this one later.

I lived in New York for fifteen years and I was often so busy with work I didn't partake in all the things the city had to offer. In the final months before I left, I started to really SEE my city.

Today, see your town. Attend a show or do something that is quintessentially that town. Don't let life pass you by. Before you know it, you'll be moving or the kids will be all grown up and you'll wonder what happened to your life.

There's a reluctance to going out that can sometimes birth isolation. Maybe you're someone for whom this isn't a problem. But maybe you are someone who puts other people first and who makes excuses on why you can't go. Tonight, go!

"Get out from your house, from your cave, from your car, from the place you feel safe, from the place that you are. Get out and go running, go funning, go wild, get out from your head and get growing, dear child."

- Dallas Clayton

JOURNAL

DAY FIFTEEN

Discover a New Poet

It's easy to stay within one's comfort zone. The books we like to read, the artists we enjoy, the people we surround ourselves with. While it feels wonderful to know what you appreciate, you may be closing yourself off to other perspectives and ways of seeing that could truly change your life.

Today, discover a poet you've never heard of before. You may dislike poetry and have not one book of poetry in your possession.

To find a poet you can do the usual means of discovery: library, on-line, a friend's bookshelf, a bookstore. Whatever the case, take your time. Like any genre there are also subgenres and styles of poetry that are drastically different from each other. There are the beats, the Nuyorican poets, classical works, modernists, limericks, elegies, sonnets, haikus, and narratives, to name a few. Who will you discover today?

Your life is your life
don't let it be clubbed into dank submission.
Be on the watch.
There are ways out.
There is a light somewhere.
It may not be much light but
it beats the darkness.
Be on the watch.
The gods will offer you chances.
Know them.
Take them.
You can't beat death but
you can beat death in life, sometimes.
And the more often you learn to do it,
the more light there will be.
Your life is your life.
Know it while you have it.
You are marvelous
the gods wait to delight
in you.
   - "The Laughing Heart", Charles Bukowski (4)

JOURNAL

DAY SIXTEEN

Don't Look Down...

Look up! So often we gaze steadfastly in the direction that we are going. More often still, we look down and hurry through the multitude of faces and scenery that are our everyday experience. Missing the nuance, ignoring our surroundings, and pushing forth as if getting to the finish line would bear sweeter fruit than the present moment we are in.

Today, I dare you to take in all that is around you. Take note of the trees and flowers, the faces, the buildings. Pay particular attention to what is above and beside you. Notice the light and the form.

Whether you are in a city or countryside, bear witness to the life that pulsates and beckons you to notice what is all around. Contemplate a tree. Consider the geometry of a house. Notice a petal, a fragment, a bird. Enter the wild and be unforgivable with your gaze. Soften the back of your neck. Inhale. And take it all in.

JOURNAL

DAY SEVENTEEN

Medicinal Makings

There are so many beautiful herbs, plants, leaves, and roots on this planet. We live in a time where plant remedies are easily accessible. You need only walk down the supplement aisle in a health food store to see turmeric, holy basil, ginger, St. John's wort, cat's claw, and a host of other medicinal remedies.

Today create your own herbal concoction. It can be anything. A tincture, a juice, an herbal infusion, a tonic, or a salve.

You can make it as involved and time consuming as you like. Think about what you want to create and also what you might need.

General instructions:

Tinctures: a clean and sealable glass jar, alcohol, food grade vegetable glycerin, or apple cider vinegar, and the herbs of your choosing.

Salves: beeswax, coconut, or olive oil, dried herbs and/or essential oils of your choosing.

Body mists: distilled water, witch hazel, spray bottle and essential oils of your choosing.

Tonics: juice or strain desired herbs and citrus, add sweetener, blend and strain, place in glass with still or sparkling water.

Herbal teas: dried or fresh edible herbs, flowers, roots, and leaves, hot water, a cup.

Room temperature herbal infusion: glass jar, herbs and spices of your choosing, let stand 15 minutes, partake. I made this one with tea roses, cardamom pods, and fennel seeds as an Ayurvedic liver cooling blend.

Happy creating!

DAY EIGHTEEN

Enter a Church

For some of you this may be very easy. Perhaps you attend church regularly, perhaps you grew up in a religious household and decided at some point it wasn't for you, perhaps you never have and never want to.

Religion and the spiritual trajectories of religious communities are extremely diverse and hold a lot of power and weight. Today's exercise will ask you to suspend your beliefs, regardless which side you fall on.

Today you are simply honoring the magic of a space. Do not deny what it may bring up for you, but also allow yourself to enter with an open mind and an open heart.

If this is a usual occurrence for you, I encourage you to see something different in your experience.

Pay attention to the forms, the light, the people. It can be particularly impactful if you are alone and during a time when there is no service.

"I like the silence of a church,
before the service begins,
better than any preaching."

- Ralph Waldo Emerson

JOURNAL

DAY NINETEEN

Chewing Meditation

Prepare yourself for a potentially profound, possibly annoying, disgusting, enlightening, and humbling experience.

I am very captivated by meditation in general. Perhaps because I decided long ago that I'm awful at it. Sitting cross-legged and in silence has always been difficult for me. That belief has led me to try various forms of meditation,

Today, try a chewing meditation. This meditation is powerful for the mind and the body. Digestion begins in the mouth, so as you can imagine, taking that much time and care sends a powerful message to the body.

On August 8, 2014 I tried this for the first time. I followed the instructions by Jay Michaelson. (5) The experience was very calming. I'm curious how you will feel. If you're moved to, record what you discover!

JOURNAL

DAY TWENTY

Won't You Be My Neighbor

Some of the best experiences I've ever had were communing with my neighbors. There is a lightness about it. Perhaps a memory of how people used to engage. Nowadays we are more and more removed from the people we coexist with.

One becomes accustomed to the reclusiveness we are often prone to in a big city or even small town. We become alone in public and in private. But being with people and sharing time is deeply important for our souls.

Today reach out to a neighbor. Create a project, invite them over for dinner, do a puzzle. Go out or sit on the front stoop. A conversation with nothing else planned! A simple act. Engage, be present, and listen. There are so many possibilities when we get together.

DAY TWENTY-ONE

Dealer's Choice!

What is it you've always wanted to do? To try? To be? Treat yourself. And listen to that inner beckoning. I realize this can be tricky. An improv game is always more efficient when there are parameters. But today there are none - release the rope. What is your dream?

It may be a restaurant that takes two months to get in. It may be reaching out to your estranged sister. It may be returning to that unfinished novel you always said you'd write.

Today, begin that journey. If it happens that you can execute it today, great. If it requires more time, great. Allow the impetus of this challenge to guide you into action.

Nothing is impossible. You know this. If you're reading this, you know this. Do it now.

JOURNAL

DAY TWENTY-TWO

Make Bread

Today put your kneading skills to work and make bread!

Whether you are gluten-free or not, egg-free or not, dairy-free or not, there is always a way to create bread. Even if you're grain free, there are seed and nut breads.

This challenge may require a little research and legwork but so worth it!

Get those paws wet and make some bread.

If for some reason, you cannot partake of bread, create and make it for someone else. It's all about flexing new muscles. And if you can partake, you're in for a treat!

JOURNAL

DAY TWENTY-THREE

Paying Homage

We move through time, create time, construct time. It exists and does not exist. Today honor someone who has touched your life.

Sit, take a breath, and see who comes up. It may be someone living or passed on.

Bad memories may surface, good ones too. Regardless, allow yourself to simmer in the beauty that is honoring someone who has left a mark.

Drink water and take care of yourself. Memories hold energetic power that can dehydrate and exhaust you.

You are held and with your tribute they will feel honored and hear you.

JOURNAL

DAY TWENTY-FOUR

Take a Hike!

Today journey forth into unfamiliar terrain. Seek out dirt and mud and hills and rock. Of course, know yourself and your limitations. Whatever and wherever the journey, may it be a time away from the usual riff-raff. Find trees and paths and the water's edge. Near you there is a territory that beckons to be discovered. It may be a path less traveled or a commonly traversed ridge. It may be an hour away by car, a half day, or a mere train ride away.

This may require a little planning (because of work or kids or a million other things). If so, earmark this page and plan the hike before you conclude this book.

Your hike awaits, don't keep it waiting... The hills are alive with the sound of music after all. Go forth!

JOURNAL

DAY TWENTY-FIVE

Sound Mapping

Sound mapping is a digital technology that records what a specific location sounds like. The objective is to record an environment's soundscape. While this is being used to educate people and give future generations the opportunity to hear what an environment sounded like, it can also be used as a meditation exercise. Sound mapping in this way is without the digital recording technology and only requires you to sit and allow the sounds in.

When I tried it for the first time it proved very relaxing and brought awareness to both my outer and inner body.

Today take fifteen to twenty minutes to simply sit and notice what you can hear. Near and far. Record what you discover.

JOURNAL

DAY TWENTY-SIX

Art and Sky

So often we ignore what is all around. The sky, the trees, a girlfriend's smile, a hat left on the table. So many seemingly inconsequential things. So much taken for granted or easily glazed over.

Today take note of what is all around you. Faces, leaves, buildings. Take photos of what moves you. It can be anything. Then find a piece of art that mirrors that image. If you prefer, begin with the painting or work of art then venture out to find it's likeness. Notice the similarities. The empty spaces. The lines.

Write about what you find – or allow the images to speak for themselves.

You don't need to be an artist to appreciate art. You need only be a human, having a human experience. Open your eyes to what is all around and note the resemblances.

JOURNAL

DAY TWENTY-SEVEN

Ya' Dig

Today dig your hands in dirt!

I lived in New York City for fifteen years and never once planted anything. When I look back, I'm not sure why. I remember talking about how great it would be to have flowers on the fire escape or an herb garden outside my apartment window. But besides planting some strawberries for a friend I never did it for myself.

I grew up in San Francisco and as far as I remember I never planted anything there either. It's very possible I did, as gardening was my grandmother's favorite pastime and I was with her all the time, but I cannot recall. She was always in the backyard tending to the flowers and vegetable garden. She was such an incredible human being. Full of spunk and love and fierce kindness. She planted a tree for every grandchild and great-grandchild. I decided when I moved back to California that I would dig my hands deep into dirt and learn to plant and reap and sow.

Today dig your hands in dirt. Whatever that means to you. Plants seeds. Plant garlic cloves. Create compost. Harvest herbs and leaves from a friend's garden. Whether at home or at someone else's house or garden, learn something new today and get dirty!

"To forget how to dig the earth and to tend the soil is to forget ourselves."

- Mahatma Gandhi

DAY TWENTY-EIGHT

Nature Persists

Notice where nature emerges today. Notice where life blooms and forces entry. It may be from gutters, from rock, from concrete. See the beauty – everywhere.

If you're moved to, take a photo. Or just take it in.

"If you truly love Nature,
you will find beauty everywhere."

- Vincent Van Gogh

JOURNAL

DAY TWENTY-NINE

Wabi-Sabi

Wabi-Sabi is a tradition of Japanese aesthetics that acknowledges, creates, and accepts the imperfection in objects and things. It is at once a philosophy and a way of life. Art too, has been built around this concept. Simple, rustic, asymmetrical, and handmade are some of the elements that may go into wabi-sabi. The transience and imperfection of life is also wabi-sabi.

Today find something in your house or in the world that possesses this discord.

This exercise might be easy for you if you already find imperfection beautiful. But for those of you that can't bare a cracked plate or the frown of a stranger, I encourage you to see the beauty in the imperfection that is, indeed, all around us.

I think of wabi-sabi when I hear someone say of their beloved husband who has passed, "I really miss the way he brushed his teeth" or "ate his food"… "it used to drive me crazy".

I have a scar right in the center of my nose. When I was asleep once and just an unwitting teenager, Zac, my first love, popped a zit on my face. For those of you who are poppers (which I was not), it was NOT ready! I was so upset and always hated the imperfection of that scar. When he died my perspective changed. It became a reminder, a talisman, an opportunity to accept all of me, even an ugly little scar right in the center of my face.

Happy hunting (within and without). You are profoundly imperfect and beautiful.

"There is no excellent beauty that hath not some strangeness in the proportion."

- Francis Bacon Sr.

JOURNAL

DAY THIRTY

Six Degrees

"I read somewhere that everybody on this planet is separated by only six other people. Six degrees of separation between us and everyone else on this planet. The President of the United States, a gondolier in Venice, just fill in the names. I find it extremely comforting that we're so close. I also find it like Chinese water torture, that we're so close because you have to find the right six people to make the right connection... I am bound, you are bound, to everyone on this planet by a trail of six people."

– Ouisa Kitteridge from *Six Degrees of Separation* by John Guare (6)

Today seek out someone you've always wanted to meet. It may not be accomplished today but the journey begins now. Who is that someone you've always wanted to see or talk with? Someone who inspires you. Someone you admire. Someone you know but lost contact with and haven't seen in years? What are your six degrees?

JOURNAL

Afterword

You've completed your first 30 days, now what?

I believe once an exercise has been learned and the muscles are accustomed to the new movements one is then ready to continue to expand their muscles and, in this case, minds even further and deeper. Ultimately, we need to be able to do this on our own, in relation to another, or in a group. I find accountability is key. My Something.New.Every.Day handle on Instagram provides me a certain level of accountability, as I've committed to posting my experiences publicly. While I often post in clusters, each daily experience is recorded and cataloged with a brief description, date, and day. Yes, that's ALL Virgo rising behavior.

If you feel different after this journey and sense that the awareness these activities awakened in you is something you'd like to continue, I'd like to offer up something my dear friend John created that we are calling The Becoming Present Process. I hope this provides you with some insights into how to walk through your days anew.

Here is an example of how John brought awareness, acceptance, appreciation, alertness, and amplification to his experiences and then acknowledged what to remember, replay, or reject in order to give his brain the opportunity to frame his experience and ultimately bring greater joy and meaning into his life.

The Becoming Present Process
5 A's & 3 R's Example

7:00 am July 25, 2012
Beautiful, mild, sunny summer day.

"I'm heading down to the Hudson River near the George Washington Bridge for my 4½ mile walk from 185 to 145th Street- Riverbank State Park and back.

I am purposefully **alert** to the opportunities nature offers this day and I go off the sidewalk to a rocky lookout spot I have frequented many times. This time- still alert to opportunity- I take a side trail that leads to a huge rock that I scamper up and sit down. I become **aware** of my surroundings by meditating with my eyes open and shutting down stray thoughts. I **accept** into my mind and body the beautiful sight of the Palisades and the sun dappled waves, the slight discomfort of the striated rock on my bottom and, most of all, the wonderful, swirling breeze on my face, arms and legs and I **appreciate** the uniqueness and specialness of the ever changing breeze. Later, as I am walking again on the path, I reflect on the breeze's touch and **amplify** my feelings by thinking of many silent birds making the breeze a celebration of the freedoms of nature.

I will **remember** this encounter as I have journaled it here and will **replay** both in my memory and when I encounter other, interesting breezes in the future. While not important to this story, I probably did **reject** the feeling of discomfort sitting on the rock. The experience and its record in my memory will undoubtedly affect my future moods, personality and preconceptions."

– John Miller

The Becoming Present Process
5 A's & 3 R's Definitions

Alert- actively and purposefully looking for stimulating opportunities with a bias towards the pleasant. Primary influence on mood and preconceptions.

Aware- observing every feeling and thought associated with the experience.

Accept- just letting the feelings and thoughts be without interpretation or judging.

Appreciate- reflect and find the beauty or specialness of the situation by bringing logic/reason into the mix.

Amplify- zero in on the essence, key feature of the experience and enhance it with your imagination. This done both during and after the experience has passed. This, at its best, is a feedback loop between emotions/feelings and reason.

Remember- replay and store the experience and your impression and reinforce them by journaling.

Replay- come back to the memory frequently, read the journal, add new interpretations.

Reject- discard, diminish information that does not enhance the memory of the experience.

The Becoming Present Process
5 A's & 3 R's

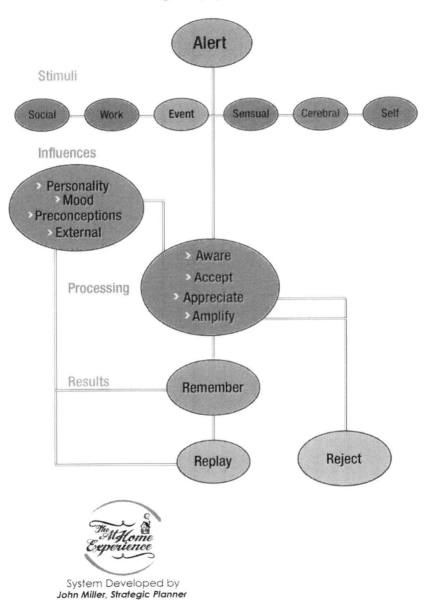

System Developed by
John Miller, Strategic Planner

From here to there is a mere moment in time and space. A metaphorical and sometimes literal jump into the unknown. Once you've made the jump, I believe, you are unable to go back. Your constitution has shifted. Your awareness has expanded and you will no longer be able to fit into your old mind-space.

May your journey take you into the most profound nooks of your soul. Until next time.

"So here's to life
and every joy it brings.
Here's to life
for dreamers and their dreams.
May all your storms be weathered.
And all that's good get better.
Here's to life.
Here's to love.
Here's to you."

– Phyllis Jean Molinary (7)

Links & References

1. **Kaypacha quote.** Mystic Mamma (2018, November 22) Weekly Guidance from Kaypacha: Open it wide and step outside. Retrieved from: bit.ly/SNEDref1

2. **Smile, smile, smile.** Alidina, S. (2015, October 2) Dalai Lama: Smiling more important than meditating. Retrieved from: bit.ly/SNEDref2

3. **Plan a Trip.** Herreria, C. (2016, June 6) The Happiest Part of your Vacation Isn't What you Think! (Huff Post) Retrieved from: bit.ly/SNEDref3

4. **Discover a new poet.** Bukowski, C. (1996) The Laughing Heart from Betting on the Muse: Poems and Stories (Black Sparrow Books, formerly Black Sparrow Press)

5. **Chewing Meditation.** Michaelson, J. (2014, August 8) Eat Your Way to Enlightenment (Huff Post) Retrieved from: bit.ly/SNEDref4

6. **Six Degrees.** Guare, J. (1990) Six Degrees of Separation: A Play (New York, Random House)

7. **Here's to Life.** Sung by Shirley Horn with arrangement by Johnny Mandel. Music by Artie Butler and lyrics by Phyllis Jean Molinary. Retrieved from: bit.ly/SNEDref5

About the Author

Chantel C. Lucier, NBCR, RM, CMT, was born in San Francisco to an eclectic family of Mexican, Norwegian, and Italian performers and musicians. She carries a BA from Mount Holyoke College and an MFA from the Actors Studio Drama School in New York.

While Chantel followed the family tradition and became a dancer, singer, and actor, she moved to New York City in 2001 and discovered the myriad benefits of reflexology and reiki. In 2007, Chantel became a national board certified reflexologist and soon thereafter a reiki master.

Her company, The AtHome Experience, is dedicated to educating and enlivening the individual towards a greater connection to themselves, each other, and their community. Through sessions, classes, videos, and books, The AtHome Experience empowers people to create and sustain optimal health. While reflexology is a specialized field, Chantel shows us how the techniques can be easily learned to use at home. By caring for ourselves and each other, we construct and co-create a better future.

While maintaining good health and caring for one's self and others is foundational to happiness, Chantel also realized that spurring creativity and new understanding of the world around us also is crucial. And thus, she has been exploring something new every day since 2014. The resulting experiences and awakenings were transformational and profound, and they inspired her to share a journeying guide for others.

Chantel has been featured in numerous articles and television/video programs, including Gwenyth Paltrow's GOOP, Jill Urban's Wellness Report, Organic Spa Magazine, Well & Good, New You, Yahoo Beauty, the Dr. Steve Show, and Howcast's 50+ DIY videos on reflexology. She shares videos on how to care for oneself and others using reflexology on her YouTube channel: YouTube.com/chantellucier.

To learn more about Chantel and her work, visit TheAtHomeExperience.com. To see her adventures in doing something new every day, follow her on Instagram @Something.New.Every.Day.

Something New Every Day

Made in the USA
San Bernardino, CA
23 December 2018